D1065433

B-1B LANCERS

BY JACK DAVID

BELLWETHER MEDIA · MINNEAPOLIS, MN

Are you ready to take it to the extreme?
Torque books thrust you into the action-packed
world of sports, vehicles, and adventure. These books
may include dirt, smoke, fire, and dangerous stunts.
WARNING: read at your own risk.

Library of Congress Cataloging-in-Publication Data

David, Jack, 1968-
  B-1B Lancers / by Jack David.
     p. cm. – (Torque. Military machines)
  Includes bibliographical references and index.
  Summary: "Amazing photography and engaging information explain the technologies and
capabilities of the B-1B Lancer. Intended for students in grades 3 through 7"–Provided by
publisher.
  ISBN-13: 978-1-60014-258-1 (hbk. : alk. paper)
  ISBN-10: 1-60014-258-3 (hbk. : alk. paper)
  1. B-1 bomber–Juvenile literature. I. Title.
  UG1242.B6D375 2009
  358.4'283–dc22   2008035634

This edition first published in 2009 by Bellwether Media, Inc.

The photographs in this book are reproduced through the courtesy of the United States Department
of Defense.

Printed in the United States of America.

CONTENTS

THE B-1B LANCER IN ACTION

A B-1B Lancer cruises toward a terrorist camp at the speed of sound. Its wings are swept back and its jet engines roar. Suddenly, an alarm sounds in the cockpit. The enemy has fired a **missile** at the plane. The Lancer's crew releases **countermeasures** to confuse the enemy weapon. The missile locks onto the countermeasures and explodes harmlessly.

★ ★ ★

5

The Lancer arrives at the target and releases a guided bomb. The bomb locks in on the terrorist camp. A ball of flame rises as it strikes.

The B-1B climbs higher into the sky and heads back to base. Its mission is a success.

STRATEGIC BOMBER

The B-1B Lancer is a **strategic** bomber that can fly at **supersonic** speeds. It's the United States Air Force's fastest bomber plane. It can fly more than 900 miles (1,450 kilometers) per hour. The B-1A Lancer was introduced in the 1970s to replace the older B-52 Stratofortress. The improved B-1B followed in 1986.

★ ★ ★

Pilots sometimes call the Lancer the "Bone." The nickname came from the plane's original name, the "B-One."

The B-1B Lancer is the U.S. Air Force's main long-range bomber. Its **variable-sweep wings** and powerful jet engines give it the maneuverability of a fighter plane. It can also carry heavy **payloads** of bombs and missiles.

The B-1B is the U.S. Air Force's only variable-sweep aircraft. Its wings tuck in tightly to the main body for high-speed flight. They stretch out for takeoffs, landings, low-speed flight, and high-**altitude** flight.

WEAPONS
AND FEATURES

The B-1B Lancer can carry and deploy a large payload of weapons. It has three bomb bays to carry weapons, as well as six **hardpoints** on the wings. It carries 2,000-pound (900-kilogram) MK-84 bombs. It also carries the GBU-31 guided bomb.

A **global positioning system (GPS)** guides the GBU-31 toward targets. A GPS also guides many of the Lancer's missiles. The AGM-158 JASSM is a powerful long-range air-to-ground missile with GPS guidance.

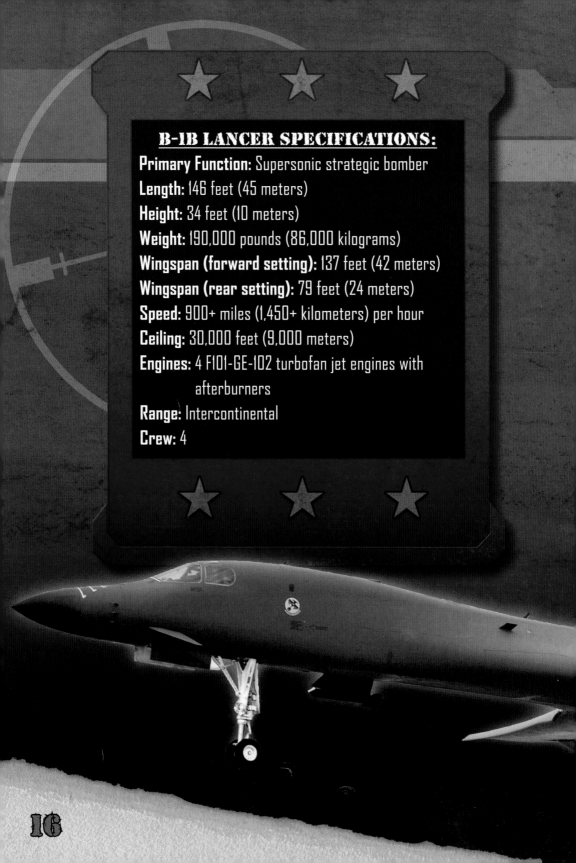

B-1B LANCER SPECIFICATIONS:

Primary Function: Supersonic strategic bomber

Length: 146 feet (45 meters)

Height: 34 feet (10 meters)

Weight: 190,000 pounds (86,000 kilograms)

Wingspan (forward setting): 137 feet (42 meters)

Wingspan (rear setting): 79 feet (24 meters)

Speed: 900+ miles (1,450+ kilometers) per hour

Ceiling: 30,000 feet (9,000 meters)

Engines: 4 F101-GE-102 turbofan jet engines with afterburners

Range: Intercontinental

Crew: 4

The Lancer has advanced systems for defense as well as attack. Its **electronic jamming** equipment disrupts enemy communications. The ALQ-161 system detects enemy **radar** and releases countermeasures to protect the Lancer from enemy attacks. The Lancer's advanced radar system can map terrain. It can also detect incoming weapons and dangerous weather.

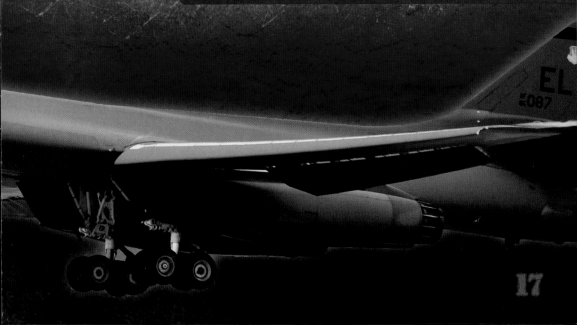

★ **FAST FACT** ★

The B-1B is not a stealth plane, but its features make it hard to detect. Its slim body and the way air flows through its engines make it hard to spot, compared to other planes of its size.

B-1B MISSIONS

The B-1B Lancer's variable-sweep wings make it capable of a variety of missions. It can carry out quick, low-altitude strikes or long-range, high-altitude strikes. It can attack targets on land or in the water.

★ **FAST FACT** ★

In 2008, the Lancer became the first plane in history to reach supersonic speeds using a synthetic (non-natural) fuel.

A crew of four operates each Lancer. The pilot and co-pilot fly the plane and navigate. An Offensive System Operator (OSO) is in charge of the plane's weapons. A Defensive System Operator (DSO) handles the plane's jamming equipment and ALQ-161 system. The crew works together to complete their missions and get home safely.

GLOSSARY

altitude—the distance above sea level

countermeasure—a defensive device, such as a flare, designed to confuse the guidance system of an enemy weapon

electronic jamming—the act of using electronics to interfere with enemy communications

global positioning system (GPS)—a device that uses satellites in outer space to determine the precise position of an object on the globe

hardpoint—a connection on a plane to which weapons or other equipment can be attached

missile—an explosive launched at targets on the ground or in the air

payload—the weapons and equipment carried by a plane

radar—a sensor system that uses radio waves to locate objects in the air

strategic—designed to reduce an enemy's military power

supersonic—able to move faster than the speed of sound

variable-sweep wings—wings that can be moved to a forward or rear position; the forward position gives the best stability at low speeds, while the rear position allows for the highest possible speed.

TO LEARN MORE

AT THE LIBRARY

Braulick, Carrie A. *U.S. Air Force Bombers*. Mankato, Minn.: Capstone, 2006.

Stone, Lynn M. *B-1B Lancer*. Vero Beach, Fla.: Rourke, 2005.

Zobel, Derek. *United States Air Force*. Minneapolis, Minn.: Bellwether, 2008.

ON THE WEB

Learning more about military machines is as easy as 1, 2, 3.

1. Go to www.factsurfer.com.

2. Enter "military machines" into the search box.

3. Click the "Surf" button and you will see a list of related Web sites.

With factsurfer.com, finding more information is just a click away.

INDEX